Octo-Oliver was an eight-armed trickster,
mingling in town,
ready to flip the
human world upside downward.

With a fast-track dash,
the octopus arrives,
eyes wide open for urban city dives.

hahaha
hahaha
hahaha
hahaha
hahaha
haha
hahaha
ha
hahaha
hahaha
With one word squirted out,
he knew how to draw a crowd,
bringing friends together
with lots of laughing, like loudly.

On a plush couch he finds
his place comfortably,
blending in the function
with tentacled grace lovingly.

A motley crew of partygoers came and appeared,
each drawn closer by the octopus's cheer.

Strobe lights and neon lights,
bouncing rhythmic beats,
he danced about vigorously
throughout the city's streets

Through the whirlwind of the party scene, he navigates with wittiness and a vexatious sheen.

With a playful squirt,
and a slyly stupid grin,
he pulled party pranks
that made people
scratch their chin.

Friends were gathered round,
intrigued by his style,
forming strong bonds
that stretch a mile.

In a haze of smoke,
he ponders life,
with philosophical musings
cutting like a knife.

Lost in his own mind,
he fumbles, juggles
and stumbles. Transforming
common life confusion
into comedic jumbles.

Deep thoughts begin to
bubble up, as he ponders
his existence with
his grip onto a cup.

As the crowd grew, the octopus was tested. And through his own antics, the people were interested

Excitement builds as the
night draws near, with
challenges ahead
to be faced without fear.

Lights flash, music booms,
as the octopus takes
center stage inside
that crowded room

There was a sudden twist,
a fight broke out quick
no bouncers in the party,
so the melee stayed lit.

CHILL YALL!
With agility and wit,
Oliver settled the
affray, turning hostility
into a playful display."

The night ended cool
with a triumphant flair,
and the octopus proved
he had skill while over there.

In the aftermath, he reflected
on his bonds, cherishing
friendships that
it fondly responds.

can i spend the night with yall?
Sure Pal
Long story short,
the party was successful.
The next step was Octo-Oliver
asking for a place to be restful.

And Oliver did this
after every single party.
Crashing on the couch
of the hosts, not feeling sorry.

That was the octopus's hustle.
Partying and lodging.
Dodging responsibility for himself
and basically squatting.

A pretty fair trade,
a party performance
for a place to stay.
If the octopus didn't
go to parties, he
wouldn't have anywhere to lay

The End.